12 Simple Tips & Tools to Help Your Grieving Child

What I Wish I Had Known When My Son Died

Mel Erickson

Copyright © 2021 Mel Erickson

Copyright Information

12 Simple Tips & Tools to Help Your Grieving Child

What I Wish I Had Known When My Son Died

All rights to this publication are reserved. No part of this book may be copied, stored in a retrieval system or transmitted in any form whatsoever or by any means: electronic, mechanical, photocopying, microfilming, recording or otherwise without the express written permission of the author in advance.

This publication is written to provide general information and guidance on the subject matter covered. The views expressed are solely those of the author and not intended to be an alternative to professional medical or psychological consultations.

Please respect my work.

Mel Erickson

For inquiries, sales or permissions requests, please contact the publisher: Mel Erickson. www.kidtalkgrief.com or mel@kidtalkgrief.com

Printed in the United States of America by Amazon KDP.
First Edition - 2021.

Copyright © 2021 Mel Erickson

ISBN: 978-1-7365868-3-9

www.kidtalkgrief.com

Dedication

Drawn by Caleb, age 6, in April of 2020

His dad is a paramedic. His mom is a nurse. He waves goodbye and says, *"I love you! Don't get the crony virus!"*

This book is dedicated to all the first responders, the last responders in the funeral profession, and health care professionals who valiantly and tirelessly serve their fellow man during the COVID-19 pandemic, and to the children who worry and have been, or will be left behind.

It is also dedicated to the parents and caregivers who are taking action to help bereaved children through their grief.

Contents

Title	Page
Title Page	1
Copyright Information	2
Dedication	3
Contents	4
Call to Action	5 - 7
Why This Book?	8 - 10
About the Author	11
A Closer Look At Grief Itself	12 - 13
Children Grieve	14 - 16
Is My Child's Grief Normal?	17
How Children Grieve Differently Than Adults	18 - 21
Insights From Hindsight	22 - 27
How To Break Tragic News To A Child	28 - 29
Watermelon Hugs	30
12 Actionable Tips	31 - 42
12 Simple Griefwork Activities	43 - 55
Not-So-Simple Tips & Tools	56 - 57
Book Resources #1	58
Book Resources #2	59
Online Resources	60
Thanks For Reading This Book	61
Newsletter Sign Up	62
By The Same Author	63
In The Same Series	64
Reviews	65

Call To Action

At this exact moment, I am grateful for you. Yes, you. Why? Because you are reading this. You are seeking to equip yourself to be the caring presence that a bereaved child needs. You are preparing to act. Thank you!

You may be wondering how to break bad news to a child, or if your child's grief is "normal." You may be struggling to know the "right thing" to say. You may want to help your child but have no idea where to start. You may be desperate for more help. I promise some answers will follow. I will be sharing with you what I wish I had known after my son died in 1983. The conversation will get personal.

Childhood bereavement is a critical issue.[1] Why? Unresolved childhood grief is a significant cause of problems in school, mental health issues, teen depression, substance abuse, risk taking behaviors, and suicide. The death of someone in a child's family of origin before the age of ten has a lifelong impact and forever scars a child.[2]

Based on CDC data collected 2013 to 2017, an estimated 1 in 14, or 5.2 million children in the U.S. have already experienced the death of a parent or sibling before they reach the age of 18.[1] These statistics do not account for the number of children who lose a "parental figure," such as a grandparent or other relative that provides care. Nor do they reflect the devastating impact of the Covid-19 pandemic's rising death toll.

The pandemic has pulled me out of retirement to educate and support the helpers of grieving kids. You and I can make a positive difference. This book is designed to better equip you to be a caring presence, and you will acquire simple activities and games to help you engage and support a bereaved child. It is going to get personal. Just imagine you are sitting with me in a comfortable setting having a conversation or a *"fireside chat."* I will be doing all the talking. Thank you in advance for listening. Thanks to technology, someday I may be able to hear you too.

If you are grieving, even though I am keeping this short, it may be too much information for you to take in at one sitting. Grief depletes our brain power. A widow once said to me, "The day my husband died my brain went on vacation. Is it ever coming back?" It makes you wonder! The answer is, **yes**, but probably after checkbook mistakes, missed appointments and assorted faux pas that will make good stories later.

Meanwhile, please be patient with yourself. Take in what you can, and come back for more later. There is a child who needs you just as you are right now, broken-hearted and dysfunctional from grief as you may be. Grief has changed you and the child. "Normal" to grief is not the normal you used to be. If fact, we would be very worried about the things we are experiencing, if they were not explained by grief. Things like sleep and appetite changes, low energy, time warp, inability to focus or remember, or a short fuse to name a few.

One more thing: be your authentic self. I am sharing insights with you that would have been meaningful to me when I was newly bereaved. They may not hit the target for you because you and I are unique individuals. We have different personalities, unique stories and loss histories, distinctive coping styles, varied support systems, alternative daily realities. Our grief is diverse and unique to us as a person. Additionally, your grief is constantly changing. A good day can deteriorate. A bad day can get better. Living in the moment takes on new meaning.

Not only are we and our grief different, but we may also speak a dissimilar language of feelings. My intent is to give you language as a <u>starting place</u> for your understanding and talking with a child. Take my thoughts or ideas, if they work for you, and make them your own. You may worry about saying the wrong thing to a child. I certainly have. But I have also learned if your heart is in the right place, if your intent is kind, children are very forgiving and are open to "re-dos."

I am calling you to action because you have a child grieving a death who needs adult support.

It may very well be a time when you may barely be able to function yourself. Both from experience and years of observation, I know that you *"fake it until you make it."* You are an award-winning actor while earning your Ph.D. in *"the school of hard knocks."* I applaud you. Go for it! Be gentle with your expectations of yourself. Love overcomes a lot of mistakes.

It is at times like this, during emotional pain, I cannot imagine not being a Christian. Knowing God and my interactive relationship with Christ through prayer and Bible reading are my personal lifeline and anchor. I am grateful for the strength, comfort, peace, and hope God gives me and for what He has done and continues to do in my daily life. What a difference it makes to live with the assurance of life in God's presence when this earth life ends. During this time of the pandemic, with both political, and cultural turmoil and uncertainty, there is peace and comfort in knowing that my trustworthy God is in control and I have a heavenly destination. Pointing you and your bereaved child to the gospel where you can find the same, is the best resource I have to offer you.

Please visit my website to learn more. www.kidtalkgrief.com.

---

1. See www.judishouse.org/cbem

2. *The Loss That Is Forever: The Lifelong Impact of the Early Death of a Mother or Father by Maxine Harris, Ph.D.*

Why This Book?

I was a grieving child. I was four when Grandma Stock who lived with us disappeared. (She went to the hospital and died. I was not included in her story.) When I was twelve, my only brother was killed in military service. I remember grownups asking me how my parents were doing, not how **I** was doing. I remember a visitor commenting how "*kids bounce back*" when my heart was breaking. I remember finding my dad sobbing in the garage. He was working on the boat my brother built in high school wood shop. I did not want to add to daddy's pain, so I left with my own. Dad died of cancer when I was sixteen, a junior in high school.

My kids were grieving kids. They were five and ten years old when their 15-year-old brother, Don Paul, died after a twenty-two-month battle with brain cancer. They still remember having hamburger hash for dinner once or twice a week. It was all their mom could think to cook. (Truth be known, it was a challenge for me to stay clean and fed, much less keep a schedule and be a wise and wonderful mom. If only I had known then what I am about to share with you now!)

After Donny's death, my passion was, and still is, helping children grieve. The best way I know to help children in this era of the pandemic is to help you.

After retiring, I volunteered as a GriefShare facilitator at my church. GriefShare is a wonderful 14-week faith-based curriculum offered by churches across the country. (www.griefshare.org.) Over the last six years I have revised and expanded my own **Kid Talk Curriculum** which I used for over 20 years in hospice and public-school settings. It now includes a faith-based component. It supplies lesson plans and supportive materials for 28 hours of direct grief support for children and includes over 100 interactive activities.

The full curriculum with the *Our Story* **Memory Book** is now available on Amazon as **Kid Talk, A Faith-based Curriculum for Grieving Kids.** Learn more at the end of this book.

In the light of the Covid-19 pandemic, I recognize the obvious:

#1 Now (Start of 2021) is not a time when we can safely meet with a group of children, *and*
#2 Grieving adults need a simple, hands-on, actionable guide for supporting the bereaved children in their lives. This is what follows.

To paraphrase Mr. Rogers, *"Making difficult matters mentionable is the best way to make them manageable."* I would add, regardless of our age. A native American saying puts it a little differently; *"If you can give it a name and a shape, it no longer has power over you."*

I believe that this underlying reality for you and me is why the Bible bids us to *"pray without ceasing."* We are created to need to externalize our feelings in healthy ways to best deal with them. It is also important that we are heard and validated. Our goal in supporting grieving children is to help them tell their story and express their feelings around a death. It is especially important we listen to children, so they know we *hear* what they are trying to communicate.

Who is listening to **you**? It is equally important for *you* to be heard, tell your story, and talk about what you are experiencing. Your child heals in direct proportion to how you are healing.

I am a follower of Jesus Christ with a Biblical world view. I would not be giving you *"the full meal deal"* without including what I see as the vital role of faith in the healing of grief. There is plenty you can do to help yourself and your child without the faith component. Please know, however, in my 35 plus years of doing this work, I have not witnessed profound grief *"heal clean"* without forgiveness. Both the ability to forgive and hope, come in knowing God through the Holy Bible and an intimate relationship with Him. The assurance of a heavenly afterlife adds quality to this life for adults and children alike.

I told you our conversation would get personal! I do wish it could be less one sided. Perhaps I will get to listen to you someday. I would like that.

Connect with me at mel@kidtalkgrief.com.

Meanwhile, may these insights and practical tips & tools give you confidence to be a caring presence and healing influence for a child you love.

About the Author

Mel Erickson BA, CT (ret), received her training and experience, working as a social worker and bereavement coordinator for hospice. In 1997 she co-founded a non-profit serving the bereaved community as a resource for education and support. Mel received National Professional Certification as a Bereavement Facilitator from the American Academy of Bereavement in 1996 and was Certified in Thanatology: Death, Dying and Bereavement by ADEC (Association for Death Education and Counseling) in 2003. Her passion was coming alongside children who had experienced a death.

She co-authored *Teen Talk, An 8-week Curriculum for Grieving Teenagers*. She wrote the ***'Our Story'* Memory Book** as a tool to help children tell their story and process their grief. As a presenter, she has spoken and delivered training internationally. She has coordinated the GriefShare ministry at her church and more recently has returned to her passion of working with grieving youth.

During the COVID-19 pandemic, Mel is focusing on education and support for caring adults who want to support bereaved children. To that end she has recently published two books, a newsletter and launched a website.

Mel and her husband have lived in Tacoma, WA since 1976. Three adult children and two adorable grandchildren enrich their lives.

Learn more at www.kidtalkgrief.com.

A Closer Look At Grief Itself

Grief and mourning are our natural, inherent healing responses to separation and loss. When you think about it, *every change is a loss* because when something new begins, something else ends. A child lives with big losses (death of a person or pet, divorce, moves) and small losses (schedule change, loss of a toy, no school). We struggle more with changes we did not choose. Currently we are all living with uninvited changes due to the pandemic and lots of unknowns. We are also living with "anticipatory grief," if we have loved ones who are ill or at risk, wondering who might get sick and die because so many have. Grief is a stressor. Many are struggling to "hold a lot of balloons underwater:" finances, employment, schooling, childcare, inflation, healthcare, lifestyle changes and grief. Whew!

I want to emphasize it is important to recognize that grief is a natural human response to separation and loss. It impacts every aspect of our lives, our physical self, our emotions, our thinking, our relationships, and our spiritual self. It depletes us – our physical, mental, emotional, and spiritual energy. We experience changes in ourselves we may not attribute to grief. For example, the inability to concentrate, a short temper, a short memory, change of appetite, and many more. It can be frightening because we have never felt like this before. This is true for children, teens, and adults. We are just not ourselves. Yet, I have come to see grief as a God-given healing process, even though we hate it. We heal by going <u>through</u> the process. In fact, the only way out of it is through it. The journey is different for everyone. It is not short and sweet. What matters most is we *choose to lean into it* rather than run, hide, evade, or stuff it. The good news is there are lots of things we can do to help ourselves move forward. Those things are called griefwork. Every one of the **12 Actionable Tips *(Page 31,)*** is griefwork.

You and I are doing griefwork with this conversation. It may have made you cry. That is OK. We need to *"cry until we are dry."* Here is a little jingle that I learned years ago. It is quite a profound truth.

Tears on the outside fall to the ground
and are slowly swept away.
Tears on the inside fall on the soul
and stay and stay and stay.

There is a lot to learn about grief. I am still learning. I encourage you to learn as much as you can, as much as your grieving brain will let you take in. The reason is *the more you do griefwork and intentionally work at healing, the better example you set for your children.* Healing is a choice. You are a role model. It is not optional. I will include a list of books and websites that can help you better understand your own grief. There are online support systems and social media support. Be wise and selective, but do not think you must do your grief journey alone. You and I were created to be in relationship with people and with God. We were created to heal and grow. Be patient. (Haven't I said this before?)

Children Grieve

The range of feelings and expressions of grief is necessary to the healing process at any age. Each child's grief is unique due to many influences: his or her personality, developmental stage, family dynamics and history, support systems, culture, religion, environmental stressors, and cause of death. A child's grief looks different at different developmental ages. His or her grief will look different when the death occurs and subsequently. Just like adults! Yet, children grieve differently than adults do because they are kids. The following is a general list of "normal behaviors" (meaning **not unusual**) you might see in a grieving child:

Regression
Changes in eating and sleeping pattern*
Insecure or clingy
Nightmares
Difficulty concentrating*
Afraid to be alone
Afraid of the dark
Cries more often
Headaches or stomachaches*
Hyperactivity
Preoccupied with death and/or health*
Speaks of decedent in present tense
Lack of emotions
Withdraws from friends*
Takes on role of decedent
Irritable moods*
Acting out or sassy
Suicidal thoughts*
Fatigue or loss of energy*
Angry towards parents or siblings
Non-compliance
Discipline problem in school
Guilt about words or actions
Magical thinking (unrealistic explanations)

*There are so many variables in children's grief behaviors, it is hard to describe a "typical" child's grief reactions. The behaviors with asterisks need monitoring as explained in the first paragraph of the chapter: **Is My Child's Grief Normal? Page 17.**

This list would have any parent worried. Remember, "*normal*" to grief is not the pre-grief status quo for anyone in your family. I have not given you a list of normal adult grief experiences because we are focusing on children. However, I recommend that you look at Therese A. Rhando's, list of *"Appropriate Expectations You Can Have For Yourself In Grief." (Please see Book Resources 2, page 59. List available at* www.kidtalkgrief.com.*)*

Hopefully, finding yourself in her list will reduce your concerns about your own grief and allow you to lean into the process less stressed. I have found Rhando's list to be helpful to many grieving adults over 30 years!

You do not need to be reminded your "*normal*" is out the window for your whole family. You and your child or children have entered a season of grief. "*Lean into it*" rather than resist it so that you both get *through it* in the least amount of time possible. It will still feel like it is way too long. People often ask, "*How long will this last?*" The truth is "*as long as it takes.*" My smarty-pants answer is, "*Too long!*" because that is how it feels.

The key to remember is grief lasts for a season during which a large part of it, in the beginning, is a roller coaster ride. Its intensity and intrusiveness diminish over time. Be clear that to heal does not mean that you forget your person who died or stop loving him or her. It means you will find purpose and joy in living again, though your life will never be quite the same.

Your grief will recycle and always be a part of you because you loved or were attached to someone who died. You will be changed, potentially for the good, and you will grow as a person. You will be setting an example for your child or children.

This can be a time when you rely and grow in your faith and relationship with God. Even if you are mad at Him like I was. Nothing compares to His love and the peace, comfort and hope He will give you and your child.

Is My Child's Grief Normal?

Probably so. You will note the list of "normal behaviors" may not be characteristic of your child before the death. Extreme behavior changes lasting over an extended period would be a flashing yellow light. Family, friends, or a teacher may express concern to you. If physical and emotional symptoms persist over time or interfere with daily functioning, seek a professional evaluation. *Watch particularly for the items on the previous list that have asterisks.* Look for a professional who is experienced in working with grieving children. A child who did not have behavior issues before the death is likely to work through their grief with support and guidance. That said, if the death was sudden, unexpected, or violent, it is always wise to seek a professional assessment and guidance for the child and the whole family.

Keep in mind that a child who is acting out more after a death than before it happened, may have underlying fear and anxieties in addition to his or her grief response. Remember the questions of death. (**Actionable Tip #8, The Difficult Questions Page 39.**) Have those important conversations. I repeat, the more unknowns you can remove for a child, the better. Do be sure you are gentle and sensitive to the child's readiness to know. Listen, listen, listen, and observe. Respond in a way that the child knows you *hear* them. For example, "I think you're telling me _____," or "The way you are behaving makes me think that you are feeling _____, or thinking _____, am I understanding you?"

Do an internet search for *"children's grief support"* to locate specialists or a program in your area. I have compiled lists of books and internet resources in addition to what you will find in the back of this book *(Pages 58 & 59)* that you may find helpful. You will also find them on my website at www.kidtalkgrief.com.

Here is a bit of good news: As you do griefwork with your child, you are also doing your own griefwork. It is a win-win!

How Children Grieve Differently Than Adults

#1. Delayed grief response.

It is not uncommon for a child to not display grief behaviors for four to six months, or even a year, after a death. *"Gone"* is an abstract concept, as are negative numbers. That is why algebra is not offered until after middle school. It takes time to absorb the reality of gone and not coming back. I clearly recall feeling a stab of pain and an intake of breath when remembering my son was gone months after he had died. One of the biggest tasks of griefwork is to absorb the reality of gone. A reality we do not like or want. A first-grade girl came to Kid Talk. She was biting kids at school. Her mom had died the previous year and her dad had remarried. The night we talked about anger, she scribbled with a red felt tipped pen on newsprint until she made holes in it. Then she tore off pieces, chewed them up and spit them into the waste basket. (*The pens were labeled non-toxic!*) Her father reported that she never bit again. She literally needed to get the mad out.

#2. A child's grief symptoms may mirror ADD and ADHD behaviors.

Signs of Post-Traumatic Stress Disorder may be seen in children (and caregivers!) after a death from a long-term illness and prolonged suffering. Patient observation is needed as well as caring adult support. Feelings need expression to dissipate. We need to cry until we are dry. We tell the story over and over in many ways until the telling does not feel like new news. Children may not have words. They express their feelings with behavior and through play. We can support them by giving them multiple ways to make their feelings visible and by teaching them the language of grief. The activities you find here will help you with this. These activities are a simple beginning. There are lots more when you are ready to explore or have a friend explore for you. I describe **103 activities** in **Kid Talk – A Faith-Based Curriculum for Grieving Kids** *with Our Story* **Memory Book.** You can learn more about it at the end of this book *(Page 63,)* or on my website.

#3. Magical thinking may be the child's erroneous way to explain what has happened.

Children need to make sense of what has happened and fill in the "WHY?" blank, just like adults. However, with active imaginations and a sense of guilt, they may come up with explanations that are far from reality. Therefore, it is important to tell them the truth, as difficult and painful as it may be for you. With magical thinking, the child believes his ideas, thoughts, actions, or words have influenced the course of events in the death story. It is how a child may link his inner, personal experience with the external physical world. An eleven-year-old boy came to Kid Talk and explained to the group that he had an argument with his dad before school, which was why his dad had a heart attack. He had bad dreams about alligators under his bed. It took gentle repetition of the doctor's explanation of his dad's health condition for this child to let go of his self-blame. In doing so, the alligators also left. This is a classic example of the power of a child's magical thinking.

#4. Kids do not sustain emotional pain as long as adults can.

Kids remain kids, even when their hearts are broken. They may be sobbing one minute and asking to go outside and play the next. They need to take breaks. They need to release energy and emotions with activity, physical play, and exercise. (*Think of a puppy!*) It is the "*teachable*" moments when we want to be a caring presence for a child. They happen most often in the car and at bedtime. Family mealtimes are important for this reason. Again, this is not easy if you yourself are grieving. It helps to remember a child will grieve in small increments over time. His grief will recycle with sights, sounds, smells, and special occasions, just like an adult's. Try to keep your antennae tuned and observing for little windows of opportunity to clarify magical thinking or invite expression of feelings. Remember to model expressing your own.

#5. Kids will recycle their grief as they grow up.

Particularly in their teen years when their abstract thinking matures. The stories and memories will need to be revisited and made sense of. It is most helpful to have a memory book to trigger the buried or forgotten emotions and grief responses. I often hear children say, *"I'm afraid I will forget ."* A memory book is reassuring. The more we can help a child express their grief in childhood, the less likely he or she will be to experience trouble with school, depression, rebellion, and risk-taking behaviors as a teen, known consequences of unresolved childhood grief. There is an assortment of memory books online. I really like mine, of course. It is currently packaged with **Kid Talk - *A Faith-Based Curriculum for Grieving Kids*, (See Page 63,)** so that you get instructions that help you maximize the memory book experience for the child.

#6. Children may instinctively not want to add to their adult's emotional pain.

Remember my story about finding my dad sobbing in the garage? I have seen that dynamic over and over. Kids protect their parents from their own emotional pain, which is sweet. It also means they may be vulnerable to grief vomit. (**See Hindsight #6, Family Plan for Grief Vomit Page 24.**) It may explain why adults do not know about a child's magical thinking that perpetuates emotional pain.

#7. Kids may not have words, but they will do griefwork through play and art.

Be sure and have lots of art supplies. Choose to talk about the person who died. Let the conversation lead to memories and perhaps inspiration for a drawing. Feelings can be drawn or painted. Play dough can be shaped and pounded. My favorite play dough is homemade. The recipe is on the website at www.kidtalkgrief.com. Making it can be a great togetherness activity.

#8. Some kids regress, and some become little adults.

Some kids do neither. Watch for change. Delegate, if you possibly can, to another adult, family, or friend, what you may need to, so a child can still be a child while grieving. For example, a young son may assume the role of *"the man of the house."* Or the oldest child may assume care for the younger siblings. This is not a fair or reasonable expectation. You may have some very mature conversations. Let your child know you intend to cover the parent role, even though you are a bit of a mess right now. Suggest you will all work together for the time being, but you are still the parent. Of course, you are grateful for his love and support, but you want him to still have a childhood. Together you will first get through this crisis *season* of survival, then you will all begin to heal and grow as you do your griefwork.

Insights From Hindsight

More Things I am Glad I Learned After my Son's Death

Children generally grieve in direct proportion to how their caregivers are grieving. They take their cues from the adults in their lives. We are role models at a time when we may not be high functioning ourselves because we, too, are grieving. This is our reality. It is not an easy assignment. Here is more of what I have learned:

Hindsight #1. Educate yourself about what normal grief looks like for you and your child.

Your understanding about the grieving process makes it easier to lean into it rather than shy away from it, and resist the discomfort and emotional pain. Remember, we are afraid of the unknown and we may never have felt like this before. Remember, also, grief is a healing process. The more you do your own griefwork, the more you are helping your child. This might be the third time I am saying this. It is so important.

Your family and friends may benefit from a better understanding of grief also. It might help them know better how to support you. Share this book and other books or articles. This is a win, win. There are resources for you at the back of this book and on the website. www.kidtalkgrief.com.

Hindsight #2. Tell the truth.

Children are resilient and can handle almost anything as long as it is the truth, and they are supported in love with lots of listening and comforting touch. Truth telling builds a foundation of trust that is desirable to have as the teen years arrive. It is natural for us to want to cushion the pain for our child. But it is best your child hears the truth from you and knows questions and discussion are always welcome. Whether you tell them or not, they will eventually learn what happened one way or another.

They may overhear adults or other children talking. Lies or incomplete truth about the cause of death complicates a child's grief and damages their trust in you. Use clear, simple language as much as possible to tell the story, then wait for the questions. The child's version of the story will most likely be revealed in several small increments over time, such as while driving in the car or bedtime. Expect repetition. Gently correct mistaken understanding and magical thinking. It will probably take multiple reviews. Both children and adults may have to learn to live with not having all the answers we would like to know.

Hindsight #3. Clarify with your kids that grief is a family affair.

You might say, "We are all impacted and will respond in different ways at different times to_____'s death. We may not be ourselves for a while. We may cry a lot. We may be noticeably short tempered or easily frustrated. It is important we <u>all</u> understand there is nothing we cannot talk about, meaning we can talk about anything. Let's plan on it!"

Hindsight #4. Tears may be missing or we may have "dry tears."

You might say, "We may have short fuses and frustrate easily. Beware of "'gunny sacking'" mad and sad. Sometimes what we need may be a good cry. What movie makes you cry? Sometimes we need a good explosion! What can you do to get the mad out? Tear up an old phone book if you can find one, junk mail if you can't? Draw a picture and throw marshmallows at it? Yell? Outside please. Smash ice cubes while you are out there. What matters is, *we are in this together*. We will figure out together how to get through this because we are here for each other. We will do griefwork together. We will also each need to do griefwork on our own in our own way. We will give each other space and make allowances for "'*not normal*.'"

Hindsight #5. Our family ground rules have not changed.

You might say, "We are still loving and respectful of one another. We say please and thank you.

We tell the truth. (I will answer your questions with the truth!) We let each other know where we are going and when we will return-or ask permission as appropriate. We will have dinner together. Food quality will eventually improve. Count on it!"

Hindsight #6. Acknowledge with the family that "grief vomit" happens: our plan.

Try this explanation. "It happens in grieving families. Grief vomit is when something angry or unkind erupts out of your mouth. You were not expecting it. If I pointed my loaded "*'you gun'*" at you and said, "'You never ...'" or "'You always...'" or "'I hate ...'" etc., these are examples of grief vomit. Of course, the tone of voice can be grief vomit too, as can our body language and behavior.

"This is how we, as a family, will deal with grief vomit:

"**Step #1**. We will respond with "*ouch!*" This is how <u>all of us</u> will respond to being hurt by grief vomit for at least this next year. If it is the next day when you figured out something said was hurtful to you, you can still say, "ouch!" You might say, "Remember yesterday when you said.... OUCH!"

"**Step #2.** After "ouch!" is when the offender/shooter/vomiter labels his or her words as *"grief vomit"* and says, "That was grief vomit. I am sorry. May I take it back?"

"**Step #3.** is to answer, "YES!" *Unlimited takebacks* are going to be how we roll while we are getting through all our messy journey through grief."

This grief vomit/ouch! drill may seem unnecessary and silly. Even so, it works. Choosing to say ouch!, label grief vomit and give unlimited takebacks sure did help my family. You cannot feel angry and silly at the same time. It is like a brain toggle. This new habit can keep anger from escalating into a more hurtful interaction when family members are all hurting already. It keeps the bridge of communication open with much less damage to relationships because of grief. We all need patience with one another when we are not ourselves after a death.

Patience can be challenging to come by for all ages. (This is another reason to make sure everyone in the family is getting adequate sleep, nutrition, and exercise.)

Grief Vomit and Toilet Bowl Love really do go together. (Grief vomit may need to be flushed!) The grief vomit 3-step strategy is for family and personal peace, while toilet bowl love is very personal. It can, however, impact relationships significantly. (***See Activity # 10, Toilet Bowl Love Page 51***)

Hindsight #7. Ask the child if he/she/they have any questions about the cause of death.

Ask if they would *tell you* the story as they understand it. Remember children are susceptible to **magical thinking** and will fill in blanks with false information in trying to make sense of what has happened. Make sure, gently and simply, that a child has all the facts straight.

It is so important to clear up magical thinking. We want to remove any unnecessary burden of blame and guilt that a child may be carrying. It may take more than one conversation.

Hindsight #8. Kids need a "connecting link" with the decedent.

A connecting link or continuing bond is something concrete in the child's possession that reminds them of the decedent. It may be something that once belonged to the decedent such as a hat, clothing, jewelry, a blanket, or a collection. Ask the child what he or she would like to have for his or her own that belonged to____. It may surprise you what the child would like as a keepsake. I was 16 when my dad died and liked to wear one of his flannel shirts. Some have made quilts or stuffed animals from the decedents clothing. Special treasures may need to be saved until the child becomes of age. A memory book or special memory box can be particularly comforting.

As mentioned, I often hear from children that they are afraid they will forget the person who died. It is wonderful for the child to have their own photo album, memory book, or a photo with the decedent that is theirs to keep - maybe in their room. Writing out stories to go with the photos is excellent griefwork.

Note to grandparents: Are you taking photos of your interactions with your grandkids? Keep your own scrapbook that you can then pass along. An old-fashioned scrapbook or a digital delight. You can even add a personal letter or your ethical will. Why not? Create a legacy while you can!

Hindsight #9. Grief is a stressor.

Everything you know about stress management applies. Talk as a family about what we can each do to take care of ourselves when we are overwhelmed with too many *"alligators nipping at our heels,"* or from trying to *"hold too many balloons under water."*

Ask the child what they like to do to "feel better." Here are some suggestions:

play electronic games
play with a pet
bike ride
play sports
play outdoors
walk
deep breathe
talk with a friend on the phone
play with toys
snuggle or hug
social media
color or "do art"

A teen may want to just be with friends or listen to music in their room. Mom may want to take a walk, take a nap, or read a book. Dad might want to read the sports page or watch TV.

So, you are stressed because you are grieving. You are just ducky. (***See Activity #2, Just Ducky Page 45.***) Friends say, "Let me know what I can do to help." They may or may not call again. They pick up their empty casserole and disappear. (*It is called "the last casserole syndrome."*) You do not know what to ask for, or maybe not even what you need.

It is hard to ask, even when you know what would help. Give yourself permission to delegate. I have put a list on the website of things that people could do for you. Use it. ASK! You will also find a Holiday Checklist that will help you decide what is important to your family this year and how you may choose to simplify. You can be on sabbatical from "*normal!*" *(www.kidtalkgrief.com.)*

Hindsight #10. Deep Breathe.

Make sure everyone in the family knows how to deep breathe. It is the best calming tool I know, besides prayer. Learn three or four kinds of deep breathing and practice them together. Do deep breathing together after a grief vomit episode! Deep breathing can stop a meltdown when you are in public. It can wake you up if you are driving tired or sleepy. Do an internet search on **Deep Breathing**. I love Body Flex taught by Greer Childers because it is multi-purpose: aerobic, toning, strengthening, pelvic floor toning, and stress managing – not to mention hilarious. Look up her **Body Flex Introduction on YouTube**. Try the "monkey face" and "lion face" with your kids. Have a good laugh while you practice stress management AND get fit!

How To Break Tragic News To A Child
FOUR IMPORTANT STEPS

This is where it starts: the tragic news. These steps, by the way, are appropriate for adults too.

1. Give a warning. "I need to talk to you. Can we sit down, please? I have sad news to tell you." Words to this effect allow for an inner bracing. Remember getting called into the principal's office? You thought, "Uh, oh! Not good." You were "braced" for a potential emotional assault.

2. Tell the story. Using age-appropriate language, start the story from the beginning and lead up to the tragic outcome. Keep it short, simple, and **true**. For example, "After dropping you off at school this morning, your mom was headed for the gym, like always. Unfortunately, a truck ran through a red light and crashed into your mommy's car. The ambulance came. She was rushed to the hospital. The doctors and nurses did everything possible to help her, but she died. Her body doesn't work anymore."

3. Be a caring presence for the emotional fallout. Listen, hug, touch, cry together as appropriate to your relationship with the child. Answer questions as best you can. "We will find out more" or "I will ask," are reasonable responses. Be sure to follow up if you say you will.

4. Offer next steps. What will happen next? Bring a sense of order and safety by offering a plan of action. (Also known as a Plan of Care.) For example, "Your dad is still at the hospital. Your Aunt Judy is on her way here to pick you up and take you and your sister to her house."

It is helpful to have someone close to the child present for some sense of security when their world has just been turned upside down.

Perhaps you can ask the child, "*whose hugs feel the best?*" (It could be the decedent. Hopefully, the child can name another person or two.) Try and include the best hugger in your Plan of Care. Talk with the child about how you could make that happen. Consider the child's life story. Who does the child know and trust? Who is safe? Uniting a child with the family may not be the greatest source of comfort for the child.

Listen and answer with the truth. *(Please see Actionable Tip # 1, Page 31.)*

WATERMELON HUGS

My friend wrote a poem about hugs that I really like. It is called "Watermelon Hugs." Soon after a death might be a great time for a family to adopt the code, "**watermelon**." Here is the poem:

Sometimes I'm sad;
I mean very-very sad.
Sometimes I'm mad;
I mean very-very mad.

Sometimes my feelings
Are in a jumbled-up way;
But my words get stuck
And I don't know what to say.

I need a secret word
That I can softly say
To let my people know
"I need some hugs today."

There's flipper-flap and snipper-snap
And blueberry and baba-bee;
But WATERMELON seemed just right--
It's the best secret word for me.

I shared my secret word
with some special people - just a few --
So, when they hear WATERMELON,
They will know just what to do.

Now when I'm sad and want to hide
Under my fuzzy bear rug,
I just whisper WATERMELON,
And I get a great big HUG!

By Carol Weedman Reed 2010 Printed by permission

12 Actionable Tips

#1. Answer questions with the truth and then listen.
It is important to answer a child's questions <u>as they come up and when they are ready for the answers</u>. Listen, listen, listen with all your antennae. Because children may not have words, we "listen" by observing their body language, behavior, and their moods. We note changes. They may be able to draw their feelings or concerns. To listen is <u>not</u> to problem solve. That is not what is most needed. Being heard and understood is. Feelings do not fix. They just are. Reflect to the child what you think he or she is feeling. He or she will correct you if you have not got it right. When you do "get it," they are no longer alone feeling that way and may be able to move on. For example, instead of saying, "Don't feel that way." You might say, "You are feeling bad because you were mean." Feelings are not right or wrong. They just are. What we <u>do</u> with our feelings is what matters. It is OK to remind a child of this. You might even ask if they have an idea about what they could do with their feelings. Or would they like to hear suggestions? (Draw a picture, write a letter, smash ice cubes, apologize, go outside and scream?)

At some point it will be important to explore the child's understanding of death. *(See Actionable Tip #3, Talk About What Dead Means Page 32.)* This conversation with a child will probably happen in bits and pieces and not all at once. There are some beautifully written books that can help you with this. I have made a list for you at the end of this book *(Pages 58 & 59)* and a longer list at www.kidtalkgrief.com.

#2. Please, use the words "died" and "dead."
Euphemisms can be misleading to a child and feed their magical thinking. Kids are literal. For example, to say "passed away" may lead a child to wonder when the decedent is coming back. You might simply ask if the child understands what dead means. In doing this, our goal is to generate understanding, minimize magical thinking, and remove

stigma from the topic by talking about it. *(See - How Children Grieve Differently Than Adults - #3 Magical Thinking Explained, Page 19 .)*

#3. Talk about what dead means.

Here is how I define dead and talk about it with a child:

"Dead means that grandpa's body does not work anymore. The doctors could not fix him or make him well. Because he is dead, he cannot see, cannot hear, cannot feel touch, cannot talk, cannot think, cannot eat, cannot breathe, and cannot pee or poop. His heart is not beating because he died. Decedent is a word we use for a dead person. Grandpa is our decedent. We will always love him, even though he is no longer here with us. (*See the insight that follows on Page 33.*)

"All living animals are here on this earth for only awhile before they die, sometimes for a little while like a butterfly, or sometimes for years and years like grandmas and grandpas. People are animals. Did you know that you are an animal? We live in an "'earth suit,'" our bodies. When our earth suit stops working, we die. When we are dead, our "'earth suit'" is empty and is no longer needed. Something needs to be done with it. I like to think of a butterfly cocoon. The caterpillar has a new life as a butterfly. Butterflies remind me of our new life in heaven. (The internet has lots of butterfly crafts for children.) The cocoon is empty and no longer needed. Period. So, something must be done with it. Have you ever had a pet die? Did you bury it in the ground? Did you have a goodbye ceremony?" We will talk about what to do with an empty earth suit in *Actionable Tip #4 on Page 34.*

This is an opportune time to talk about heaven. Here is what I believe as a Christian and words I would use with a grade school age child:

"Human beings were created by God in His image according to the Bible. So, we are much more than just our bodies. He has given us a soul and spirit also - "'the inside us.'" God created the inner part of us, like Him, to be eternal and living with Him and His angels forever in heaven. There is no pain, sorrow, sickness, darkness, or tears in heaven. God loves us so much He left heaven to be here on earth as

Jesus to demonstrate His love and provide the way for us to be with Him forever in Heaven. The most important decision we make our whole time on this earth is what we will do with our knowledge of Jesus Christ and what He did for us."

When tragedy and death happen, it may be difficult to lean into a "'loving God.'" Therefore, it is so important to know Him well through Bible stories that illustrate His love, power, and faithfulness to keep His promises. By knowing Him well, His character and His history with man as revealed in the Bible, we can trust Him - even when we do not understand why something bad had to happen. To know God more makes it easier to trust Him more and love Him back. Then we live with confidence in our future in heaven and with peace in the present.

*Insight - rarely talked about:

Not all people who die are beloved. A child may be grieving an abusive or absent parent, for example. To refer to that person as "*your loved one*" may be inaccurate or hurtful. A 12-year- old in one of my Kid Talk groups yelled, "He is not my 'loved one!' I hate him!" That is the day we started using the word 'decedent' to refer to people who have died. Understand that *we grieve the loss of a person in our lives in proportion to our attachment* to that person. Attachment has to do with their role and importance - or wished for role - in our daily lives.

Love and hate are the flip sides of the same coin. The absence of either love or hate leaves a big hole in our lives. Indifference is the absence of love. Where there is indifference, there is unlikely to be profound grief of a decedent.

This side note is to help you understand why a child (or person) who did not have a "positive" relationship with the deceased may still be grieving. In this case, "decedent" is a helpful word, even though it is not commonly used. I have learned that by using it we get comfortable with it. So do the kids.

#4 Talk about burial and cremation.

Especially if the child is a part of your decedent's story and has been or will be included in the funeral, memorial service, or celebration of life. (More about this to come.) Here are words I use with a child:

"The Bible says that our bodies return to the dust of the earth. (Genesis 3:19) It is what nature does with an empty earth suit. The word for this process is "'*decomposition*.'" It happens slowly over time by putting a body in the ground. Some families choose to put the body in a coffin and bury it in a cemetery with a gravestone designed to honor and remember the decedent. A cemetery is a special place where there are lots of graves and gravestones.

"Another way to return a dead body to dust is called cremation and it happens very quickly. Cremation means the decedent is put in a box in an extremely hot fire or furnace and is reduced to ashes. The ashes are called cremains and may be saved in a special container, sometimes called an urn. Cemeteries often have a special place to store urns in a building called a columbarium. The columbarium has a wall with many niches or cubby holes about 12" square to keep cremation urns. Each of the niches has a small marker like a gravestone to identify and honor the decedent inside.

"Do you know that cremains can be turned into beautiful jewelry? Cremains can also be divided into small containers, including jewelry, and shared with the family of the decedent as a keepsake. Some families keep the cremains or urn at home. There are choices to make.

"So, some families choose to bury the decedent, and some to cremate the body. In our family we _____. (Decedent's name) is going to be (buried or cremated). _____, (Name) is making the arrangements. We will be able to visit and put flowers there (e.g. on the gravestone or columbarium) to show our love for _____. We can also put flowers by (_____'s) photo at home. We could put a battery candle there also. Then any one of us could light it when we are missing _____ or want to send our love to him or her."

#5. Talk about goodbye ceremonies.

The following is narrative I would use with a child:

"Goodbye ceremonies or rituals are called a funeral, a memorial service or celebration of life."

(Please see the NOTE under *Actionable Tip #7, Plan and Prepare Your Child for the Service of Remembrance, Page 37.)*

"Families have different traditions about how they like to say goodbye. People who live in other parts of the world or have different religions also have their own special traditions. In our family we usually have a_____.

"At a funeral, the decedent's body is present in a casket. Everyone who comes signs a guest book. A funeral is often led by a pastor or priest. Scriptures may be read, and hymns sung. The family normally sits together in a special place. Sometimes the casket is open and sometimes it is not. Friends and family are invited to file by and say goodbye, mostly very quietly. People may cry, knowing it is the last time they will see the decedent. Funerals are typically held at the funeral home chapel or a church. (The funeral home is where a body is taken to be prepared to look nice in the casket. It is also where you buy a casket.) A photo of the decedent is often displayed. Or there may be a big poster board of photos of the decedent that tell the story of his or her life and family. Food and a reception are traditionally held after a funeral, either at the funeral location or another place such as at a home or restaurant.

"A memorial service is when friends and family gather, usually in a chapel or church, but it could be anywhere, like someone's back yard in the summer, to remember the decedent and talk about his or her life, what he accomplished and special memories. A memorial service may or may not have a religious leader, scripture and hymn singing. Otherwise, it is a lot like a funeral except the body is not present. The urn containing cremains may be placed by a photo of the decedent.

"A celebration of life is a lot like a memorial service, but perhaps more informal and very customized to the personality and style of the decedent and the decedent's family. Memories, fellowship, food, and drink are very much the focus.

I once attended a Celebration of Life where the decedent's shiny Harley was on display. He loved that machine, and it was a huge part of his life. His biker friends attended dressed in their leathers. The stories they told! He would have loved being there!"

#6. Should my child attend the service of remembrance?

Yes, with some exceptions and thoughtful preparation.

The death of a family member is part of the child's story and the child needs to be included.

Why? Because:

- being there validates his *belonging* to the family, and that he is important enough to be included in the family story

- being there helps him connect with the decedent as known by others

- being there allows him to witness grief and know it is natural to cry, for example

- being there allows him to be comforted by other people who are also sad and will miss the decedent

- being there gives him the opportunity to express his love for the decedent and say goodbye

- photos taken at the service should include the child so that when his grief recycles, the above reasons are reinforced.

I think that a child old enough to feel attachment to the deceased should attend the service. The exception might be if the child has health or emotional issues, is not comfortable with crowds or possible displays of emotions or upset people. Trust your heart to know what is in your child's best interest. The presence of children at funerals and weddings is always a challenge. However, the importance of being there **for them** is worth the planning and manpower potentially needed, in my opinion.

#7. Plan and prepare your child for the service of remembrance.

Ask a family member or friend to stay with a child to listen to and answer questions. I recommend doing this as a back-up plan, even if you think you will be OK. If the child becomes upset, the "funeral pal" can leave with the child. The pal can also assist the child with their part of the ceremony or ritual. Hopefully, the child has been invited to share, write a letter, draw a picture, or in some way (light a candle, ring a bell, place a flower) to demonstrate their love for the decedent. At the reception, you can invite the children to go outside and blow "love bubbles" for the decedent! They just speak their message, "I love you," and blow bubbles. Filling the air with love bubbles can be a family ritual at any time. (*See Activity #12, Page 54.)*

NOTE: We are all anxious about the unknown. It is especially important to sit down with a child before any first-time experience and let them know all the variables they may expect using all five senses. For example, what you might see, hear, smell, taste, touch, and add what you might feel, too. This prep talk is a good idea before a hospital visit to an ill person, before the first-time dentist visit, etc. The more unknowns you remove, the less fear and anxiety there is likely to be. Knowing they will have a "pal" to be with the whole time is also comforting. Fear and anxiety can be what is behind misbehavior. Do your best to address it. After painting a picture of what the service of remembrance may be like, if the child does not want to attend, allow that choice. Assure him that together you will find other ways to remember and celebrate your person who died.

Here is an example of a pre-funeral or memorial prep talk:

"Tomorrow we are going to a memorial service for grandpa at the cemetery chapel. I want to tell you what to expect. People you know who knew grandpa will be there. There will be a lot of people who you do not know, too. They will probably be dressed up - like for church. It might even be crowded because a lot of people loved him. Your cousin Jenny will sit with you and be with you the whole time if you want her to be. We will sit in a special section just for families. It will either be in a little side room where people cannot see us or the very front seats in the chapel. I think there will be lots of flowers, so it will smell good. We will all have a printed program to look at. It will list the order of the program and tell grandpa's story. You will hear people talking as they arrive and get settled. (It is kind of like church or a school program.) Pastor Paul will oversee the service. You can look at the program with Jenny. She will read it to you if you would like. We will probably sing grandpa's favorite hymn and read scripture. Someone will tell grandpa's life story. There will be a slide show of pictures from when grandpa was little until he got old. You are in some of the pictures! Those will be cool to see.

You may hear people cry. You might cry. I might cry. Let's remember to put Kleenex in your pocket! Some people cry softly, and some are loud and wail. I was scared the first time I heard loud wailing and it came out of my own mouth! It even scared the dog! It only lasted a few minutes. I sure felt better afterwards. I got the pain out. Don't worry, someone will be there to comfort anyone who is having a "grief attack." It happens. Especially at funerals where you may or may not see the body.

Grandpa's body will not be at our memorial service, just photos. People will be invited to share memories of him. Do you have a favorite memory of him? Would you like to draw it? We could put it in his casket later to stay with him. You could also write him a goodbye letter. Would you like to do that? I will help you. Or you could ask Jenny to help you with that.

After the service we will go into a big room where there will be lots of food. Everyone has brought something. Aunt Sue made your favorite chocolate cookies. People will be talking and telling stories about grandpa, so there may be laughter and tears both. I look forward to hearing other people's memories.

You will not have to sit still and be quiet at the reception. There will be other kids there. I don't know if there will be a place outside for you to hang out. We will find out. This is all I can think of to tell you what to expect. Do you have any questions?"

#8. Address the difficult questions that come with a death.

They are: Who is going to love me? Who is going to take care of me? Who else will leave me? Am I going to be alright? These questions are true for a child and for the child in all of us. In fact, I believe these questions, though not conscious, are a part of our anxiety generated by the pandemic. It is good to address these questions to reduce the fear and anxiety of a grieving child, both for the immediate future, e.g., your next steps as a family, and for the distant future. Remember, fear and anxiety may contribute to misbehavior.

If a parent or parent figure has died, as the surviving caregiver, have a sit-down talk as a family (I call it a *"family huddle."*) to assure the child or children you have no intention of leaving them. Here is how I would go about this conversation. (These are my words. Borrow them if you wish or just speak from your own heart.)

"Kids,_____has died because_____. I want you to know I (or we) do not intend to leave you. Well, except to go to work or to the store and stuff like that. I plan to watch you grow up and make me and _____(your dad/your mom/whomever) proud. That is why I wear a mask, fasten my seat belt, quit smoking, take my vitamins, brush my teeth, eat vegetables, and do whatever else to take care of myself. However, kids, we have learned from our sad experience that things can happen without our permission - things that we do not want and do not like. Should anything like that happen to me, God forbid if I should die, I (or we) have planned for Aunt Suzie and Uncle Jim to take care of you. They love you and would want the best for you just like I do. I have made a will, which is a legal document naming them as your guardians. I am telling you this so that you know you are loved and will always be loved and taken care of in a loving home by people you love.

"Our plan now is that I get old like grandpa was and watch you grow up, go to college, have a career, get married, have children, and make me a grandma. I love our plan! I love you! So now we move forward loving one another and trusting God to provide and take care of us as He has and will continue to do."

There is much discussion on the news and in households about the pandemic and there have been many life changes for children –

like wearing masks, staying home, no school or online school, no team sports, no outings or play dates.

I think it is important to reassure your child that you are doing everything possible to stay healthy. All of us are! Relieve this anxiety before it builds. Will you be creating anxiety where there was none? Maybe for a minute. At the end of your conversation, the child should feel loved and confident about being cared for. That is your goal. Questions may come up later. That is to be expected. Meanwhile, turn off the TV news when children are present.

If a sibling has died, the surviving children need to know they are treasured and would be grieved just as much. Say this out loud. Make it believable by lots of time spent with the surviving child or children, inviting them to express their own grief in multiple ways, hugs, and touch, and listening, listening, listening. Back to using all your antennae and observation skills. Talk about grief and how we are all changed by it, how we will work through it together, and how we intend to honor the decedent by living and loving again. Talk about grief vomit, ouch! and unlimited takebacks. ***(See Hindsight #6, Family Plan for Grief Vomit, Page 24.)***

I think it is a mistake to whisk away all the belongings of a deceased child. The message might be communicated that if you (a sister or brother) died, we would get rid of everything that reminds us of you, everything that shows you were a part of us. Go slow. Take time. Invite siblings to take something of the decedents they would like to have or keep as a *"continuing bond."* This could be clothing, a hat, book, toy, game or even bedroom. Make sure that everyone in the family is ready to say goodbye to *"more of the child"* (or person) who died. I remember how significant it was to us when a young friend took away Donny's drum set. Donny was an awesome drummer. His practicing impacted all of us! The remaining four of us stood in the driveway and watched his drum set disappear down the road. Somehow the house felt even quieter, even though there had been no drums for months.

37 years later, the drum solo of *"Wipe Out"* can still bring me to tears. ***(See How Children Grieve Differently Than Adults, Page 18,***

#5 Kids Will Recycle Their Grief, Page 19/20, and #8 Kids Need a Connecting Link Page 25.)

#9. Maintain your schedule and household ground rules.

Remember that *"normal"* to grief is not ordinary normal. Everyone in the family is adjusting to a new normal because someone is gone. No one can be the exact same person they were before the death. Consistency with the basics - mealtimes, bedtime, and general ground rules of courtesy - provides some stability and the comfort of predictability during so much change.

Of course, this is much easier said than done when you can barely remember to brush your teeth. It is OK to *ask for help* with meals, with taking the children for an outing, or engaging a child in some griefwork activities. It may be appropriate to have a friend or relative who can help in the home for a season.

#10. Tell your child's teacher, counselor, or coaches about the death.

It will help them be a caring presence for your child at school. Some kids find solace in being at school. Others may struggle to concentrate and stay on task. Either way, it is reassuring for both you and the child to know that if needed, there is someone at school who knows the story, who may make accommodations, and who may be a potential support person during the many hours each day a child is away from home. Do request confidentiality if it is important to the child.

#11. Remember special days and family traditions.

Birthdays are still important, including the birthday of the decedent. Holidays are important even though currently during the pandemic we are not able to celebrate together and be with extended family if that is our tradition. If someone has died, our holidays would be different anyway. There are resources for "How to Survive the Holidays" for grieving families. I will post some on www.kidtalkgrief.com. Hopefully, by the time you read this, I will have a teaching video for you to learn all sorts of holiday tips for your grieving family. The anniversary of a death can be particularly difficult. For all these occasions, I recommend having a "family huddle" to talk about what matters to each person and how to show love for the person who died, even though he or she is no longer here. Special occasions are a wonderful opportunity to memorialize or "make our love visible." This is an important part of griefwork. (***See Activity #12, Love Bubbles Pages 54/55.***)

#12 Affirm your faith.
This is where I would be affirming my faith and beliefs with the children. That would go something like this: "Remember, guys, we are children of God. He is our heavenly Father. He knows us, loves us, understands us, and has promised never to leave us or forsake us no matter what. He has given us the Holy Spirit to live inside of us. We can talk to Him anytime. We can read our Bibles to help us remember how much He loves us and how powerful He is to help us. He also heals our broken hearts - while knowing how much we hate how we feel right now. He gets what it is like to be sad, mad, frustrated, worried. He provides us with a safe place to rest in His presence and in the Word. You can go there on your own or we can be with Him as a family any time. How about now?"

* * * *

OK, reader friend, there is a lot more to be said. In my chat with you, I have just included a conversation I would have with my kids or grandkids. It all hinges on believing there is a God who created the universe, and that the Bible is the truest revelation of God known to man. You may or may not buy in. If you are curious, there is more on this topic - the ultimate tip - on my website. I cannot <u>not</u> offer you the path to the greatest gift ever, that is a wonderful relationship and eternal security in the presence of our loving God. Knowing God is our lifeline!

12 Simple Griefwork Activities

Each of the following activities is given a name, a supply list, and suggested narrative so you have an idea of what to say. You will need basic "*art supplies*" that include pencil, pen, crayons or markers, scissors, and glue sticks. Old magazines are good to have also. Learn "the punch lines" from me and then use your own words.

#1. My Broken Heart

Supplies you need:

- 2 pieces of 8.5" x 11" paper
- Colored paper, magazine page, newspaper, anything will do
- Scissors
- Pencil, pen, marker, or crayon Glue stick

Action: Cut out 4 paper hearts. Make them approximately 5" tall.

You and the child will each have a pair of hearts and a piece of plain paper on which you may want to write or help the child write, "My Broken Heart" at the top of the page. You may also trace the outline of the heart onto the blank page.

Narrative:
Invite the child to demonstrate how his/her heart has been broken. "Let's show each other how our hearts have been torn apart since _____ died." If doing the activity together, which I recommend, say, "You do yours and I'll do mine." They probably will not look alike because we are each unique. Allow the child to tear his or her heart into pieces. The outcome may be anything from confetti to just two pieces.

Say something like, "Ow! It hurts, doesn't it? Can you feel it? I feel it here." Put your hands where you may feel the pain of grief. "Where do you feel it in your body?" Then, "Do you think we can put our broken hearts back together? Does it look impossible? It may FEEL impossible! We know that with God, all things are possible. He wants us to heal. But we must feel to heal. It is called grief. So, let's do some griefwork that helps us heal. Ready?"

Take the remaining heart and scribble all over one side. You may choose to write words that describe the decedent on the heart. Or write what you will miss most about him or her. Then tear this heart only two or three times so that you can put it back together like a puzzle. Apply glue to the side on which you scribbled or wrote. Put it together like a puzzle.

While you are working, comment, "It sure is a lot of work to put a broken heart back together!" and "sometimes we need help putting our broken hearts back together." Ask if the child would like help. Also, you might say, "I am glad we are doing this together. We are doing griefwork that helps us heal."

When completed, again say, "Ouch! It is easy to see that our hearts are hurting, isn't it?" Then, "Do you think that our hearts will heal?" and "Will they be able to love again?" Pause for an answer. The answer is "yes," they will if we choose to do the hard (painful!) work of grief. "It is called griefwork. It means finding lots of ways to get our feelings out. How can you express your feelings? What are some of the feelings that you are feeling now?" (Sad, mad, hurt, lonely, scared, worried, guilty, love.) "How do you get them out?" Pause. "Here are some ideas: cry, draw, throw ice cubes on cement, pound a pillow, scream in the shower, talk, hug, exercise, play. You and I can do things together to help ourselves express our feelings. It will help us both!"

#2. **Just Ducky**

Supplies you need:

- Duck picture *(Download PDF at* www.kidtalkgrief.com*)*
- Crayons, markers, or paints

Action: Print a copy from the website or draw a swimming duck, showing its feet underwater.

Narrative: Looking at the duck picture, read the caption out loud or ask the child to read it. (It reads, 'Bereaved people are like ducks, above the surface looking composed and unruffled and below the surface paddling like crazy!') Ask, "Who are bereaved people?" The answer is, "Bereaved people are grieving the death of someone important to them.

"Do you know what *grieving* means or the word grief?"

"Grief is our natural reaction - everything we feel inside - to separation and loss. We grieve a lot of goodbyes. We may feel it a little or a lot. Every change in our life has a goodbye because when something new begins something else ends. The COVID-19 virus and pandemic have imposed a lot of changes on us we did not ask for. We have had to say goodbye to school as we knew it, to time with friends, to the freedom of not wearing a mask when we go out. There are so many more goodbyes we are living with, in 2021! Can you think of more?

"When someone special dies, we may feel it a lot! We are 'bereaved.'"

You might choose to add: "The more connected we are to the person who died, the more it hurts to say goodbye. Can it hurt to say goodbye to someone who wasn't nice to me? Yes, of course it can because you were "connected" as a part of your life. It is important to know that it is natural and OK to grieve the death of someone you are mad at or even hate. Forgiveness is part of our griefwork. Doing griefwork will help you (and me!) feel better. It takes time and we need to choose to do the painful work. I think it is good news we can do some of our griefwork together!

"Please color the duck so we can put it on the refrigerator. We want everyone in the family to know we may all be <u>feeling</u> more than we are <u>showing</u>. We are all "'*paddling like crazy*'" to look "'*normal.*'" Nothing feels normal now, does it?

"Sometimes when people ask us, "'How are you doing?'" to answer "'fine'" is just not the truth. How about if we say, "'Just ducky!'" It means we may look like we are doing fine, but underneath we are paddling like crazy. Grief is a major stressor. Of course, we are all paddling like crazy! This can be a code we share with the family and our friends. When we answer, "'**Just ducky!**'" they will know that we are having a hard time.

"Maybe they will offer to do griefwork with us. Or at least give us a hug. (Do you remember the code, "'**Watermelon?**'" Now we have two codes!" **Watermelon and Just ducky!**)

#3. Favorite Things

Supplies You Need:

- Writing paper

- Pencil or pen

Action: Make a list of the decedent's favorite things. For example, favorite food, restaurant, color, game, sport and team, people, place, vacation, music, car, place to eat out, holiday, book, magazine, memory, etc. You can even add pet peeve!

Narrative: "Let's make a list together of all of _____s favorite things that we can think of." Then put your heads together and think of as many favorites as you can. Consult other family members. It can be a fun family project! It will also help you make an acrostic, which is next.

What things make you think of _____? Is there anything of theirs you would like to have to keep as your own? Would you like one of grandpa's plaid shirts? Would you like to have a piece of grandma's jewelry? It is nice to have something that makes you feel close to them. It is called a "connecting link" or a "continuing bond." I have grandma's favorite bookmark in my Bible. (*See Hindsight #8, Connecting Link Page 25.*)

Bonus Idea: Cut out magazine pictures that remind you of the decedent or tell something about him or her. Glue the cutouts onto a paper to create a collage or glue them onto a shoebox and it becomes a Memory Box for connecting links!

#4. Acrostic

Supplies You Need:
- Writing paper
- Pencil or pen

Action: Use the letters of the decedent's name to create a word picture of who they were as a person. Refer to your favorite things list. Think of their character traits also. Here is an example:

BOB

Big brother, baked cookies, bossy

Outside worker, only ate vegetables

Beat everyone at card games

Narrative: "Let's use the letters of _____'s name to write down everything we can think of to describe who he was. Together we will make a word picture of him! "We will start by writing his name across the top of the page and then down the left side of the page. Then we will think of words and phrases that describe him. "We can look at our

'Favorite Things' list to help us think of things. If you want, we can ask other people in the family to contribute.

"When we are done, we can copy it to make it look special. Or we could ask someone to create a fancy document on the computer that we can frame or just put on the refrigerator or bulletin board to help us remember _____.

#5. 20 Questions Memory Game

Supplies You Need: **None!**

Action: This is a memory and talking game, great for in the car.

Narrative: "Let's play the **20 Questions Memory Game!** We will each take turns thinking of a time we did something with, _____ (the decedent).

We will each get to ask 20 **YES** or **NO** questions as we all try and guess the time you are remembering." An example of questions to ask would be "Was it before_____was born? Was it a holiday? Was it a birthday? Were we on vacation? Was it at Grandma's house? Was it during the summer?" Keep in mind that some memories may not include the youngest family member(s) because they were not born yet! It is fun to discover memories other family members, especially the kids, treasure and you as an adult may have forgotten. It may also open the door to feelings - good or not - that need to be expressed.

#6. Imprints

Supplies You Need:

- Paper
- Pencil, pen, markers and crayons
- Play dough or Crayola Model Magic

Action: While sculpting play dough, talk about ways that the decedent has made a mark on the child's life, who he is today, and who he wants to become.

Narrative: "If we push our thumb into clay, we leave an imprint. People also make imprints on our lives, some more than others, of course. Some good and some maybe not. Let's think about how _____ (decedent's name) has left a mark on all of us. For example, he loved apple pie and so do you. He hated being late and now we think of him when we are running late. He loved to hear you sing. Now when you sing you think of the songs he liked to hear. Maybe you will make him proud by becoming a singer? He always helped people. You like to help people, too. That is why we volunteer or donate. We like to do things that would make him proud of us."

One boy said that his grandma collected frogs (figurines) and now he collects frogs too. An 11-year-old girl said that her grandpa believed she could do anything. She wants to make him proud of her, even though he is not here.

This is a great conversation to have while playing with play dough or Model Magic. Invite the child to create something that reminds him of the decedent. One boy made a snowman because he visited his grandma in Alaska every summer. A second grader made a cradle, blanket and pillow. Her baby sister died.

#7 Happy Snaps

Supplies You Need: **None**

Action: In your mind's eye, visualize a scene with your decedent that makes you smile. This is a mental picture, a happy snapshot or "happy snap!"

Narrative: "Do you have a memory of _____(decedent's name) that makes you smile? Picture it in your mind's eye and describe it the best you can." My happy snap is when we were camping, and I see Donny reading a book to his little sister with her in his lap at a picnic table. One child remembered making popcorn with her grandma and no lid on the pan. Popcorn went all over the place. Her grandma laughed so hard her false teeth fell out! What is your happy snap?

#8 Bumper Stickers

Supplies You Need:

- 8.5" x 11" paper cut in half lengthwise
- Markers or crayons

Action: Draw a bumper sticker with a message that you want the world to know.

Narrative: "Do you have a message for the world about kid's grief? About your grief? About your decedent? Write your message big enough that people in a car ten feet away could read it!"
Here are samples other kids have made:

- ✓ **KIDS GRIEVE, TOO!**
- ✓ **BOYS CRY TOO!**
- ✓ **AWESOME PAPA BEAR!**
- ✓ **BROKEN HEART ON BOARD!**

#9 Grief Vomit *(Please review: Hindsight #6 on Page 24.)*

Supplies You Need:

- Lunch sack
- Markers and Crayons

Action: Label a lunch sack **'GRIEF VOMIT'** and discuss what it is and what we can do about it.

Explanation/Narrative: Please review *Hindsight #6 Page 24* to understand what grief vomit is and the three important steps that you will be taking as a family to handle it. Talk while you label the lunch sacks. One child in a Kid Talk group wrote out words that were her own grief vomit and put them into the bag. I was impressed!

I encourage you to commit to saying "ouch," labeling grief vomit, and giving unlimited takebacks for at least a year after the death, longer if deemed helpful. To repeat, the value in agreeing to this silliness is *it minimizes wounds* that sever relationships at a time when we need one another, and *it keeps anger from escalating* and doing more damage.

The truth is these steps are quite sophisticated anger management techniques. Grief and bereavement take so much of our energy. Our frustration tolerance can be low and our fuse noticeably short.

A "gimmick" like this can be a big help with peacemaking.

Remember and practice the three steps: ouch! label it grief vomit, unlimited takebacks. Include Toilet Bowl Love.

10. <u>Toilet Bowl Love</u> Another gimmick that works
Supplies You Need: **None**. (*Optional: A sound bite of a flushing toilet is fun to have. You can get one on YouTube*)

Narrative: "What happens to a toilet that isn't flushed? Gross! Right? Who needs that? When we do not forgive, we can become yucky inside with feelings we don't like, that interfere with loving and being happy. Unforgiveness left alone evolves into a root of bitterness. The remedy is simple: forgive AND '"flush."' They go together.

"We flush the words and actions of people who have wounded us. That may include a drunk driver, the medical system, a perpetrator, or a friend or relative who said something that hurt. It may or may not have been intentional. Does not matter. We still need to let it go, go, go until gone.

"Here's the deal: love is a verb, an action. When we act loving, the *feeling follows*. For example, the more we are kind and help someone, the more special they become to us. Can you think of an example?

How about when you help your sister, then she loves you back and then you love her a little more, too. You invest in her, then love her. Forgiveness works the same way. When we act forgiving (repeatedly!), the feeling will come along eventually.

Sometimes we do not even feel like forgiving. We feel entitled to be mad. It could be true. However, we are at risk of the unflushed toilet effect (yuck!) if we do not deal with the incident and our response. Let's say it was grief vomit and we already went through the motion of giving the "'take-back.'" We are still feeling it. Time to flush! (Not because we *feel* the forgiveness necessarily, but because we do not want to live with the residual ugly yuck.) There are several ways to flush:

"Just say to yourself or say out loud, "'*I am going to flush that!*'" I think it helps to pantomime pushing down the toilet handle with one hand and making a finger swirl with the other. Add sound effects. Why not? (Remember the brain toggle? We cannot feel silly and angry at the same time.)

"Alternately go to the bathroom, speak into the toilet, and flush.

"Repeat as often as necessary. That may be every time you remember. If the pain comes back with the memory, we need to flush again – as often and as long over time as it takes. (Old wounds do resurface. Grief may trigger them.) Practice it together as a family in pantomime format."

Seem silly? Yes, of course. We are making fun of a very profound dynamic. I learned it from Jesus. He tells us to forgive so that God will forgive us, and we will be able to continue our close love relationship with Him. That matters to me, a lot. Here is the deal: God created us and He knows what we need to thrive. We *need* to forgive in order not to get "'gross'" inside. It is an act of obedience. An intentional choice. I cannot tell you how many times I have had to ask God to help me <u>want</u> to forgive. I had to forgive God for allowing Donny to die. His decision has never gotten my vote, even though with hindsight I see how the detour has become the main road in my life. I have been privileged to walk beside many bereaved and witness their healing journey.

Truth? In the middle of pandemic and political realities, I am doing a lot of flushing out of obedience these days. If I think about world realities, it is easy to get upset and angry. The yuck comes creeping back. Time to flush. Then I focus on who God is and what He has promised. I count my blessings. Ah! Sweet relief. Peace that surpasses understanding.

Here is one more thing about flushing. The Bible says that when God forgives, He does not remember. Not true for us. Boy, do I remember! So, I must flush every time I remember. We all do because we are human. It is how we are made. I do not want a root of bitterness to steal a minute of peace and joy from my life. Do you?

#11. Love Letter or Good-Bye Letter

Supplies You Need:

- Paper
- Pen or pencil
- Envelope (Stationery is nice to use if you have it.)

Action: Write a letter to the decedent.

Explanation: Unfinished business is a part of grief, even if we *did* get to say goodbye. Because of the pandemic, many have been unable to say goodbye in person. Our relationship with the decedent does not end because they are no longer physically present. They are a part of who we are today, who we are becoming, and we think of them often.

Memories of them surface. Their absence makes a gaping hole in our lives. Our story with them has not completely ended. Writing a letter to the decedent may help with that. The letter is a one-way conversation with the person who died. It is also possible you have things that you need to say which are not lovey-dovey.

Your letter might include any of these things:

> **Dear Grandpa**, (for example)
> *I will always remember...*
> *I wish that ...*
> *I regret that ...*
> *Please forgive me for ... If only ...*
> *You will always ...*
> *I want you to know ...*

Narrative: "Do you know that we can still talk to _____ (decedent's name)? I think of her often and miss her. I have things that I would like to say to her. How about you? Do you talk to her in your head? I do! I even talk to her picture! Let's write a letter. Would you like to use some pretty paper? Let's just say whatever is on our heart. I can help you with spelling or even write it for you if you give me the words. You could draw a picture message if you would rather. When we are done, we will decide what we will do with it. Seal it in an envelope? Put it in your memory box? Make a photocopy to burn in the fireplace? We can write again anytime you would like to!"

#12. <u>**Love Bubbles**</u> (I just cannot leave this out!)

Supplies You Need:

- Bottle of bubbles for each participant. (1-oz. party bubbles are fine.)

Explanation:
Our love for _____ decedent) does not just turn off like a faucet. It continues to bubble up and it needs to be expressed or made visible. This is true of children and adults.

It is called memorializing. How can we do that? Here are some ideas: light a battery candle and put it by a photo, (Dollar Store votives work!) put flowers or a plant by a photo, ring a bell to send love, share memories, do an act of kindness in honor of the decedent, write a letter to him or her, draw a picture, create a memory book, do an activity you did together or that your dead person loved, do something that would make the decedent happy or proud of you, wear or carry in your pocket something that reminds you of him or her.

My favorite way to memorialize with kids is to blow "love bubbles." You can buy little 1-oz bottles of bubbles very inexpensively. Go outside and give a bottle to everyone. Invite them to speak a love message to the decedent and then blow "love bubbles." Fill the air with love bubbles! This can be done at a service of remembrance, as previously mentioned, or impromptu with family, or just two of you. The bubbles float up. Symbolically, love is on its way. This is a fun way to celebrate a life - and not just for kids! You can get recipes for "supersize bubbles" online. They are like giant hugs.

Not-So-Simple Tips & Tools

The facts and insights you have learned in our conversation are not so simple. Even so, they are intended to help you know about children's grief, words you can use, comforts you can provide or recruit another caring adult to deliver. The tools and activities will help your child express grief and move forward with the healing process. This is just the beginning of your journey through grief together.

Know there is hope for both you and your bereaved child. With support your child will live with gusto again and you, too, will enjoy life though it will never be the same. You will grow stronger through your grief. You will no longer fear the worst because you have already come through it. You will know that should tragedy strike again, with God's help you will be OK, even though you will hate the process of getting there. You will use the coping skills that you have learned when you face future challenges. You will even help support others with your empathy and compassion.

I pray that our conversation has given you confidence to be a caring presence for your child and a place to start with concrete "helps." It is not rocket science. It _is_ difficult when you, too, are grieving and very possibly "depleted" physically, emotionally, and mentally by your own grief. I honor you for making the incredible effort. Good for you! God bless you!

We can only do the best we can in any given moment. Sometimes that does not amount to much. Be gentle with your expectations of yourself. You will find a new "normal." This is where our faith comes in - a lifeline while we are in process.

As a follower of Jesus Christ, I pray that you will connect or reconnect with the living God of the Holy Bible. I repeat, to do so is the most important decision you or your child will ever make while here on this earth. Amid your pain, you can still be a seeker of truth and receive healing, comfort, hope and peace that can come to you no other way.

We live with so many uncertainties and changes in today's world. Biblical truths have held up for over 2,000 years. God has demonstrated that He keeps His promises.

A wonderful gift awaits you, made possible by God's incredible love for you. Seek it. Receive it. Walk in it. For a roadmap to get you started, please visit my website at www.kidtalkgrief.com.

Mel Erickson

Book Resources 1

There is a more complete list at www.kidtalkgrief.com.

CHRISTIAN TRADITION BOOKS FOR CHILDREN
Emily Lost Someone She Loved by Kathleen Fucci
God Gave Us Heaven by Lisa Tawn Bergren
Goodbye to Goodbyes by Lauren Chandler
Heaven for Kids by Randy Alcorn
Someday Heaven by Larry Libby
When I'm With Jesus, For any Child with a Loved One in Heaven by Kimberly Rae
Remembering My Grandparent, A Kid's Own Grief Workbook in the Christian Tradition by Nechama Liss-Levinson, Ph.D., & Rev. Molly Phinney Baskette, M.Div.

BOOKS FOR CHILDREN
A Garden Full of Butterflies by Lynn S. Combes
I Miss You, A First Look at Death by Pat Thomas
Something Very Sad Happened, A Toddler's Guide to Understanding Death by Bonnie Zucker
The Invisible String by Patrice Karst
When Dinosaurs Die: A Guide to Understanding Death by Laurie Krasny Brown & Mark Brown

BOOKS FOR TEENS
Modern Loss: Candid Conversation About Grief by Rebecca Soffer & Gabrielle Birkner
Saying Goodbye When You Don't Want To: Teens Dealing with Loss by Martha Bolton
Straight Talk About Death for Teenagers, How to Cope with Losing Someone You Love by Earl A. Grollman

Book Resources 2

There is a more complete list at www.kidtalkgrief.com.

RECOMMENDED READING FOR CAREGIVERS

35 Ways to Help a Grieving Child - The Dougy Center for Grieving Children
A Guide for the Bereaved Survivor by Bob Baugher, Ph.D.
50 Days of Heaven **(Audio Book)** Randy Alcorn Oasis Audio
Children Grieve Too: A Handbook for Parents of Grieving Children & Teens by Lauren Schneider, LCSW
Children, Teens and Suicide Loss by the American Foundation for Suicide Prevention
Helping Children Cope with Death by The Dougy Center for Grieving Children
In the Wake of Suicide: A Child's Journey by Diane Bouman Kaulen
Within Heaven's Gates by Rebecca Springer
It's Okay to Cry: A Parent's Guide to Helping Children Through the Losses of Life by H. Norman Wright
Someone I Love Died by Suicide: A Story for Child Survivors and Those Who Care for Them by Doreen T. Cammarata
Tear Soup: A Recipe for Healing After Loss by Pat Schwiebert and Chuck DeKlyen
The Year of Magical Thinking by Joan Didion
How to Go on Living When Someone You Love Dies by Therese A. Rhando, Ph.D.

Online Resources

American Foundation for Suicide Prevention - www.afsp.org- whose mission it is to save lives and support those impacted by suicide.

Bob Baugher Ph.D. - www.bobbaugher.com - is a psychologist, college instructor, certified death educator, author, and speaker. He covers a large spectrum of topics in his books, articles, and videos.

Center for Loss and Life Transition - www.centerforloss.com - Organization dedicated to helping people who are grieving and those who care for them. Dr. Alan D. Wolfelt.

Childrengrieve.org/resources - National Alliance for Grieving Children/Resources -

Counselingwithheart.com - www.counselingwithheart.com - 6 Ways to Help Children Process the Death of a Pet

CTAinc.com - www.counselingwithheart.com - Remembering My Someone Special, Grieving Journal for Kids (24 pp.)

GriefCounselor.org - www.griefcounselor.org/resources/helpful-websites/ - Center for Grief Recovery and Therapeutic Services

GriefNet.org - an internet community of people with resources

GriefShare.org - a network of grief recovery support groups around the world created and supported by Church Initiative.

Opentohope.com - Articles, videos, and podcasts about coping with specific types of losses with Dr. Gloria Horsley

National Alliance for Grieving Children - www.elunanetwork.org/resources -

has a list of helpful websites.

Supercoloring.com - free coloring pages of all kinds

Teacherspayteachers.com - Search for children's grief

The Compassionate Friends - www.compassionatefriends.org - support families who have had a child die.

Dougy.org - The National Center for Grieving Children and Families

Thanks For Reading This Book

12 Simple Tips & Tools To Help Your Grieving Child
What I Wish I'd Known When My Son Died

Thank you for joining me in this conversation.
I sincerely hope it helped you. Your honest review
will help others find this book on Amazon.

Please leave your review on Amazon.

Mel Erickson

Let's chat: mel@kidtalkgrief.com
www.kidtalkgrief.com.

Newsletter Sign-Up

Would you like more tips, tools, and resources?

If so please sign up for our FREE Newsletter

Grief Talk.

Sign Up At: www.kidtalkgrief.com

Keep up to date with the latest information and guidance. When you sign-up, we will send you a **FREE** copy of:

"*How to Break Tragic News to A Child*"

By The Same Author

Kid Talk A Faith-Based Curriculum for Grieving Kids
&
Our Story Memory Book

The two books are printed together for you to easily compile a support group program with over 100 healing activities for grieving kids. The comprehensive curriculum provides lesson plans, leader's guides, supply lists and supplemental materials for 14 two-hour sessions. The user-friendly format accommodates multiple learning styles, settings, and ages between 6 and 12 years old.

With the content of these two books, you will be equipped to offer comfort and healing to one or more children

- Easily plan and implement creative and engaging activities that promote healing in a grieving child
- Have "kid talk" language for difficult explanations related to death
- Give each child a personal memory book that will help him tell his story, express, and process his feelings of grief, and not have to worry that he will forget.
- Know where to find supplemental materials, supplies and resources

Part of the Kid Talk Grief Series

Purchase on Amazon

ISBN 978-1-7365868-0-8

In The Same Series

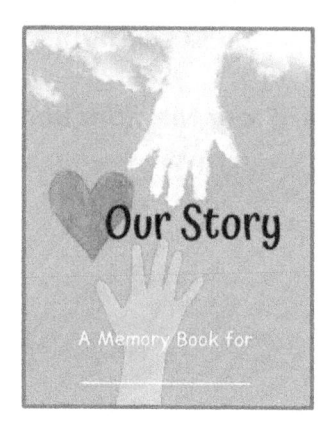

Our Story Memory Book helps the child process grief by documenting his unique story and feelings, and by lots of discussion and memorializing activities. Each interactive page is designed to foster learning, healing, and growth. It becomes a springboard for conversation, meant to promote griefwork within the family. The completed book relieves the child from worry about forgetting. It can provide needed support when grief recycles in later years.

Complete instructions and quotable narrative for each ***Our Story*** page are found in the **Kid Talk A Faith-Based Curriculum for Grieving Kids**.

Mr. Rogers said, "Making difficult matters mentionable is the best way to make them manageable." Whether parent, caregiver or professional, this companion book is a great place to start.

Part of the Kid Talk Grief Series

Purchase on Amazon

ISBN – 978-1-7365868-1-5

Reviews

12 Simple Tips and Tools to Help Your Grieving Child has everything you would need to know about children and how they grieve the death of a loved one. This includes parents, ministers, Sunday School teachers, and school counselors. Mel Erickson, the author of this all-embracing booklet, has left nothing out about how to help a grieving child. Her personal experience of childhood and adult grief will help you understand her huge heart for grieving children.

This book is a must-have companion to Mel's faith-based 13-week **Kid Talk** program for helping grieving children. I strongly recommend you use this information-packed booklet if you are a parent wanting to know more about how to help your grieving child, plan to minister to grieving children, or if you work with grieving children, this book is for you. - **Paul Conger, Grief Recovery Support Team, Lighthouse Christian Center.**

Reviewing this book confirmed to me that all the essential aspects of children's grief can be understood by any caring person, and that a caring person can really effectively help a child experiencing grief and loss. As the author states, "a child old enough to love is old enough to grieve." Being alone in grief is traumatic. This short book gives many practical tips on how to acknowledge a child's **feelings**. It shows how to give that child the needed affirmation and space to express hard emotions. Using quotable language, addressed directly to a child, this book is filled with words which can be used verbatim. This book eloquently confirms that grief is normal and that children benefit from grieving in healthy, healing ways. My hope is this book will be read and re-read by *any* family experiencing grief. - **Nanette Flynn, MPM, CT (retired)**

Many years ago, I had the honor of working with Mel Erickson facilitating grief groups for students in the public school system. Together we used many of the tools that Mel has now compiled into a "golden" resource : *12 Simple Tips and Tools to Help Your Grieving Child.* I have continued to use these timeless tools as I meet with clients individually and in group settings. The topics, discussions, and activities have worked with all ages from young children to young adults. I appreciate that these materials connect with all learning modalities. This book brings the subject matter off the page into the facilitator's/therapists hands in a beautiful way, leading to self-discovery, practical applications, and healing. The books written and compiled by Mel Erickson need to be in the resource library of every counselor working with children and young people facing issues of grief and loss.-**Lian Wolbert, M.A., ESA, Certification Attachment/Trauma Focused Therapy**

Made in the USA
Monee, IL
25 May 2023